NATIVE AMERICAN
TOOLS AND WEAPONS

Rob Staeger

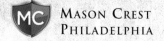

MASON CREST
PHILADELPHIA

NATIVE AMERICAN LIFE

NATIVE AMERICAN
TOOLS AND WEAPONS

Rob Staeger

SENIOR CONSULTING EDITOR DR. TROY JOHNSON
PROFESSOR OF HISTORY AND AMERICAN INDIAN STUDIES
CALIFORNIA STATE UNIVERSITY

MASON CREST
PHILADELPHIA

Mason Crest
450 Parkway Drive, Suite D
Broomall, PA 19008
www.masoncrest.com

Printed and bound in the United States of America.

CPSIA Compliance Information: Batch #NAR2013. For further information, contact Mason Crest at 1–866–MCP–Book

First printing
1 3 5 7 9 8 6 4 2

Library of Congress Cataloging-in-Publication Data

Staeger, Rob.
  Native American tools and weapons / Rob Staeger.
      pages cm. — (Native American life)
  Includes bibliographical references and index.
  ISBN 978-1-4222-2977-4 (hc)
  ISBN 978-1-4222-8864-1 (ebook)
  1. Indians of North America—Implements—Juvenile literature.
  2. Indian weapons—North America—Juvenile literature. I. Title.
  E98.I4S73 2013
  621.90089'97—dc23
                                          2013007316

Native American Life series ISBN: 978-1-4222-2963-7

Frontispiece: A collection of tools and artifacts from various Native American cultures.

TABLE OF CONTENTS

INTRODUCTION

For hundreds of years the dominant image of the Native American has been that of a stoic warrior, often wearing a full-length eagle feather headdress, riding a horse in pursuit of the buffalo, or perhaps surrounding some unfortunate wagon train filled with innocent west-bound American settlers. Unfortunately there has been little written or made available to the general public to dispel this erroneous generalization. This misrepresentation has resulted in an image of native people that has been translated into books, movies, and television programs that have done little to look deeply into the native worldview, cosmology, and daily life. Not until the 1990 movie *Dances with Wolves* were native people portrayed as having a human persona. For the first time, native people could express humor, sorrow, love, hate, peace, and warfare. For the first time native people could express themselves in words other than "ugh" or "Yes, Kemo Sabe." This series has been written to provide a more accurate and encompassing journey into the world of the Native Americans.

When studying the native world of the Americas, it is extremely important to understand that there are few "universals" that apply across tribal boundaries. With over 500 nations and 300 language groups the worlds of the Native Americans were diverse. The traditions of one group may or may not have been shared by neighboring groups. Sports, games, dance, subsistence patterns, clothing, and religion differed—greatly in some instances. And although nearly all native groups observed festivals and ceremonies necessary to insure the renewal of their worlds, these too varied greatly.

Of equal importance to the breaking down of old myopic and stereotypic images is that the authors in this series credit Native

Americans with a sense of agency. Contrary to the views held by the Europeans who came to North and South America and established the United States, Canada, Mexico, and other nations, some Native American tribes had sophisticated political and governing structures—that of the member nations of the Iroquois League, for example. Europeans at first denied that native people had religions but rather "worshiped the devil," and demanded that Native Americans abandon their religions for the Christian worldview. The readers of this series will learn that native people had well-established religions, led by both men and women, long before the European invasion began in the 16th and 17th centuries.

Gender roles also come under scrutiny in this series. European settlers in the northeastern area of the present-day United States found it appalling that native women were "treated as drudges" and forced to do the men's work in the agricultural fields. They failed to understand, as the reader will see, that among this group the women owned the fields and scheduled the harvests. Europeans also failed to understand that Iroquois men were diplomats and controlled over one million square miles of fur-trapping area. While Iroquois men sat at the governing council, Iroquois clan matrons caucused with tribal members and told the men how to vote.

These are small examples of the material contained in this important series. The reader is encouraged to use the extended bibliographies provided with each book to expand his or her area of specific interest.

Dr. Troy Johnson
Professor of History and American Indian Studies
California State University

A humpback whale. The Nootka people of the Pacific Northwest hunted these enormous sea mammals from 30-foot-long dugout canoes.

1 A Nootka Whale Hunt

The night before, the Nootka men had danced. They had danced so that they would not need to go to sea. It was time for the whale hunt, but whale hunts were dangerous. Their dance was to make a dying whale drift to shore. That way, everyone could eat and still be safe.

But a whale had not arrived.

The men stripped down and painted their faces black. They pushed their dugout canoe into the water off Vancouver Island. Their wives were not on the shore to see them go. They were at home, lying still in their beds. The women did not eat or speak. They did not even sleep. Their stillness and their concentration was another ritual. It would protect their husbands at sea.

The chief rode at the head of a 30-foot boat. The eight-man crew paddled out to sea. After a while, they spotted a whale resting on the surface. Silently, they brought the boat around behind it. As they approached, the chief steadied his harpoon. It was made from yew wood. It had a sharp tip with two barbs on it. The barbs would keep the harpoon in a whale when it tried to pull away. The barbs were nicknamed "man" and "woman."

Suddenly, the chief hurled his harpoon, spearing the whale. In

The Nootka first made metal whaling harpoons similar to the one shown here in 1803, after stealing iron from an English ship anchored off the coast.

reaction, the whale dove. The harpoon was attached to 600 feet of rope. The crew hurried to let it out of the boat. This was the most dangerous part of the hunt. The rope had to be let out quickly, yet carefully.

The harpoon line had four sealskin floats attached to it and spaced evenly along the rope. As the whale dove, the floats told the hunters how deep the whale was. As floats returned to the surface, the hunters knew the whale was not far behind.

When the whale surfaced, the hunters threw more harpoons at it. The whale dove once more without taking a breath. This happened again and again. After a few hours, the constant swimming tired the whale out. It surfaced, unable to fight any longer.

The men paddled the dugout to the dying whale. A hunter pierced its heart with a bone-tipped spear, and the whale breathed its last.

However, the hunt wasn't over. The men still had to tow the beast back to land. A few men jumped into the icy water. They slashed the whale's jaws and pushed them closed. Then they tied its mouth shut. This kept water out of it. Whales were heavy enough without filling them up with ocean water. Finally, the whale was lashed to the boat and the men began the long, hard trip home.

In the end, it is difficult to say what effect the rituals had. Did the women's stillness protect the men? Perhaps, but no one can be certain. What is clear is that the ingenuity of the Nootka helped bring the whale to shore. The dugout brought them to the whale, and the harpoon killed it. The sealskin floats helped them keep track of the whale, and the rope around its mouth kept it from getting too heavy. Nootka tools killed the whale, and Nootka tools brought it home.

Like Native Americans throughout the continent, the Nootka knew their environment. They were able to make complex tools from local materials. Native Americans' creativity in toolmaking allowed them to survive, and thrive, in harmony with the land. §

11

An Inuit fishhook. The beads, which served as a lure, were probably obtained in trade with Europeans.

The bark of birch trees had a variety of uses for Native Americans of the Northeast. Shown here is a birch bark basket.

2 Tools and Weapons of the Northeast

No matter where they lived, Native Americans made the most of their natural resources. In the forests of the Northeast, the greatest resource was trees. Naturally, there were many wooden tools. Even more than wood, however, bark provided many things to the woodland Indians.

In the summer, women peeled bark from birch trees and used it to make containers. A strip of bark was steamed so it would bend. Then it was creased and bent along the creases. When the ends met, women sewed them together. Then they sewed another piece of bark onto the bottom, making a container.

Birch bark containers had a variety of uses. Women strapped baskets called **makuks** to their waists to gather berries. Birch bark buckets were used to collect sap for maple sugar. Women also used birch bark trays to harvest wild rice. The trays helped separate the rice grains from the chaff. When the rice grains were flipped into the air, any extra particles would blow away. Grains sank to the bottom of the tray. The process was similar to panning for gold.

Birch bark was also used to make fans. A handful of feathers could be turned into a fan by stitching a piece of birch bark around the quills. Simpler fans were made by sliding a sheet of birch bark into a split twig.

Birch bark had many other uses. It was sewn into sleeping mats. Rolled tightly and lit, it was a torch. Bark was shaped into cones and made into moose and deer calls. String was made from bark fibers.

Aside from the bark, many tools were made from the wood itself. Household utensils were made from maple, birch, and elm. They were carved and scraped with bone or stone tools. Hollowed-out logs were used as mortars to crush and grind corn into meal. In the fields, people used short wooden hoes for farming. They used a wooden tool similar to a crowbar to pry up any inconvenient roots.

The Northeastern tribes' crowning achievement in wood- and barkwork was the birch bark canoe. The canoe was a boat with a wooden frame and bark sides. Because of the thick forest, it was often quicker to travel along rivers and streams. Canoers knelt on the canoe floor and paddled it forward. Birch bark canoes moved with grace and speed. They were difficult to tip. Also, they were lightweight. It was easy to carry them over shallows or to another stream. Even though they were somewhat fragile, they were easy to repair. In the forest, spare parts were all around.

In addition to travel, canoes were also useful for fishing. There were many different ways to fish. One way was to drag nets made of bark fiber along in a canoe. Fish that got tangled in the net were pulled into the canoe. It was important to clean the nets after fishing. Nets were dipped in a liquid made from sumac leaves to kill the fishy odor. Fish avoided nets that smelled.

Fishermen also caught fish using hook and line. Men drifted in canoes, dangling fishing line from their wrists. Fishhooks were made

Native Americans spear fish near the banks of a lake. The torch at the front of their canoe would most likely have been made from tightly rolled birch bark.

of bone—usually deer bone. Attached to the hook would be a torn piece of blanket as bait.

Woodland Indians also used spears to catch fish. Two different types of spears were used. Bigger fish, such as sturgeon, were speared with regular, one-pointed spears. Smaller fish were caught with a three-pointed spear called a **leister**. The three prongs kept the small fish from wriggling away.

Woodland Indians also built traps for fish. When fish swam upriver, the men would lower a frame of branches behind them. When the fish tried to return to the lake, they were caught in the frame and clubbed.

For hunting, most Native Americans used bows and arrows. In the Northeast, the best bows were made of hickory wood. Other bow woods included ash, hemlock, elm, and white oak. Bows were about four feet long and two inches wide at the center grip. The ends tapered into smaller points. Each end of the bow would have a notch in it, called the nock.

15

NATIVE AMERICAN LIFE

> **A birch bark canoe that could carry six passengers weighed only 100 pounds.**

This is where the bowstring would fit. Bowstrings were made of plant fiber or animal tendons, called **sinew**. They were sometimes even made from the necks of snapping turtles.

After a bow was carved, scraped, and smoothed, it needed time to season. The Menomini rubbed their bows with bear grease. Other tribes seasoned their bows with different oils.

Every arrow had three parts. The shaft, the longest part, was usually made of wood. It was important to choose the right wood for the shaft. It had to be sturdy enough so that the arrow wouldn't wobble, but flexible enough so that the arrow could be shot straight. Most Woodland Indians made their arrow shafts from cedar or pine.

Arrowheads—the second part—were usually made of chipped stone (mostly flint, a hard quartz). Some arrowheads, however, were made from bone or antlers. In the back of an arrow was a notch. This kept the arrow from slipping on the bowstring. Just ahead of the notch were three feathers, known as fletching. Northeastern tribes usually fletched their arrows with eagle, hawk, or turkey feathers. The feathers were dyed and then attached with sinew. Fletching was not just a decoration—the feathers helped the arrow to fly straight.

Many tribes, including the Algonquian Indians, used stone tomahawks. Tomahawks are short-bladed clubs, similar to axes. They could be thrown or used for hand-to-hand fighting. Other tribes used simple clubs made from wood, stone, or bone. Spears, of course, could be used for warfare as well as for hunting.

Winters in the Northeast were very cold. It snowed often, and the snow could get quite deep. Woodland Indians found ways of moving through the snow. Hunters used toboggans to pull their game back to camp. A toboggan had two hardwood boards lashed together. The front end of each board was curled up so that it wouldn't dig into the snow. Toboggans were not very wide, but could be up to 10 feet long. Men pulled them by a strap around their chests. Sometimes they attached them to dogs.

Snowshoes were another Native American invention. They were made by bending green wood into a loop. Beech, ash, and willow branches worked well. The front end of the shoe was round, and the ends would be tied together at the heel. The shoes were braced with crossbars to help keep their shape. A mesh of leather thongs was attached. Snowshoes made walkers' feet wider. This helped distribute their weight, thus making it harder to sink into the snow. §

17

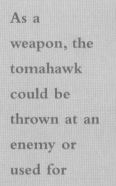

As a weapon, the tomahawk could be thrown at an enemy or used for hand-to-hand combat. Shown here is an 18th-century engraved tomahawk from an Eastern woodlands tribe.

BIRCH BARK CANOES

Birch bark canoes weren't made entirely of bark. A wooden frame was built for each canoe. The best wood for this was white cedar. Woodland Indians cut wood for ribs, crosspieces, end pieces, and the floor of the canoe.

Canoe ribs needed to be bent into shape. Boiling water was used to make the wood pliable. Water was heated by dropping hot rocks into it. The wooden ribs were soaked in the boiling water. In time, they could be slowly bent. During the bending, more boiling water was poured on the wood. This kept it from becoming too stiff.

Canoes needed thick bark sides. The thickest bark grew in the spring. To peel the bark from a birch tree, men cut a long slash up its trunk. Then they carefully peeled the bark away, prying it off with a wedge or a knife. Bark was removed down to the green rind. This became the outside of the canoe. The white, outer layer of bark became the inside.

The bark was sewn together using roots of black spruce trees. The roots were thin, flexible, and very tough. Birch bark sews together well as long as it remains wet. Once it dries, it becomes taut and firm.

The seams of the canoe were sealed with spruce gum to make it watertight. In time, the green outer layer of the canoe would darken, becoming dark brown. It could be scraped off, revealing the white bark below. Woodland Indians would scrape the dark brown layer off in elaborate designs.

NATIVE AMERICAN LIFE

Light, easy to maneuver, and quick, the birch bark canoe addressed the transportation and fishing needs of Native Americans. The canoe shown here stands on the lawn of the Grand Portage National Monument in Minnesota, the site of a former fur-trading post.

NATIVE AMERICAN LIFE

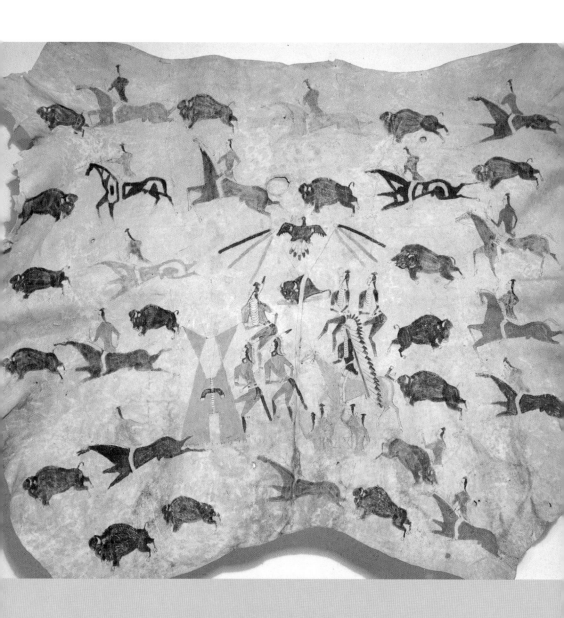

This buffalo hide robe carries
a design symbolizing harmony.

3 Tools and Weapons of the Southeast

In the Northeast, hunting provided the main source of food. In the Southeastern part of the continent, farming was more important. Tribes in the Southeast planted corn, beans, tobacco, and squash in the spring. During the summer, they fished in streams and rivers. When summer cooled into fall, it was time to harvest the crops.

Men and women both worked in the fields. They used tools called **mattocks**. A mattock is a digging tool similar to a pick. It has a flat blade at the end at a right angle to the handle. The mattocks were made of hickory wood. Some had blades made from buffalo shoulder bones.

In addition to the planted crops, river cane grew wild along the banks of streams. Cane was used for many things, including sleeping mats, drills, arrows, shields, and building materials. It was also used in basket making.

Native Americans had many uses for baskets. They were used for storage, for washing crops, as fish and bird traps, and even as hats. Baskets were made almost everywhere in North America, using different materials in each region. Southeastern basket makers were among the best on the continent.

First, the cane would be cut into strips. Often, it was dyed. The dyes were extracted from plants in the area. Bloodroot, for example, made the cane a reddish color. Black walnut wood dyed it black, and butternut dyed it a yellowy brown.

There were two basic ways to make a basket. Some baskets were plaited. This meant that the cane was woven into a thick mesh, crossing in and out. If the cane was dyed, the basket maker could make designs in the weaving pattern. The other way to make a basket was by coiling. Strips of cane were coiled from the bottom of the basket up, in a long spiral. Some baskets were coated with resin to make them watertight.

During the summer, much of a tribe's food came from fishing. Fishing was done from dugout canoes. Dugouts were different from birch bark canoes. They were made from hollowed-out logs.

Men hollowed the logs by slowly burning them away. In order to burn wood away, hot coals were placed on the area that needed to be removed. The coals would burn the wood beneath them slowly and evenly. When cooled, it was easy to dig the burnt wood out of the log. Indians used scraping tools called **adzes** made out of stone or bone. Then, more hot coals would be placed on the same area. When they cooled down, the log could be dug out even deeper.

Once the log was hollow, it was filled with heated water. This expanded the sides and softened the wood. When the dugout was as wide as it needed to be, the sides were braced with wooden crossbeams. Designs were carved on the outside. Sometimes, extra pieces were added to the front and back.

Dugouts were much heavier to carry than birch bark canoes. They

Dogs and, later, horses pulled travois, wooden frames fitted with netting for carrying supplies or sick people.

also didn't turn as quickly. Still, they were useful in catching fish. Fishermen used anchors made of stone. If water sloshed into the boat, they could bail it out using a container made from a shell. Shells were also used to make spoons, bowls, and scrapers.

Florida's Seminole Indians made excellent dugouts. They stood in them, spearing fish and alligators in the everglades. Seminole fishermen had excellent balance. Although dugouts can tip easily, the Seminoles usually stayed upright.

When moving their camp, natives of the Plains and Southeast loaded their things onto travois. A travois is an A-shaped wooden frame, fitted over a dog's back. Netting under the frame kept items from falling through.

23

NATIVE AMERICAN LIFE

By the end of the 17th century, horses—brought to America by Europeans—became more common, and bigger travois were made to fit horses. A dog could pull only 75 pounds, but a horse could pull several hundred. Travois were strong enough to carry young children and sick people. Sometimes, a travois was fitted with a shade to make the ride more comfortable.

One of the most useful resources on the Great Plains was the buffalo. Buffalo were an important source of food, of course. They also provided many things needed to make tools. Rope was made out of buffalo skin, as were shoes and clothing. Stone tips were lashed to arrows and spears with buffalo **rawhide**. Buffalo sinew could be made into thread. Its bones were shaped into many woodworking tools,

The Seminole tribes of Florida made excellent dugout canoes by hollowing out large logs with hot coals.

NATIVE AMERICAN WARFARE

North American tribal warfare was conducted mostly in quick, commando-style raids. Some tribes even carried moccasins of their enemies to disguise their tracks. Raiders stole goods and captured enemy warriors.

In some ways, Indian conflict was ceremonial. Counting coup, for example, was an important symbol of bravery. This meant touching or striking an enemy without killing him. Taking an opponent's weapon was treated as seriously as killing him. The Blackfoot word for honor in war is *namachkani*. Literally, it means "a gun taken."

When horses became common, raiding became more aggressive. War parties could move faster on horseback. Plains Indians sometimes wrapped horses' hooves in leather to muffle the hoof beats during a sneak attack. Also, horses made a tempting target for theft.

Guns made combat deadlier, but tribal warfare had already been heading in that direction. By the 1800s, scalping was common. A scalp was the flesh and hair peeled away from the top of an enemy's head. Scalps were dried and attached to scalp poles, weapons, or war bonnets. Sometimes, even women's scalps were taken. They were proof that a raiding party had made it past the defending men.

including awls, adzes, and gouges. Intestines were made into watertight jugs. Horns were carved into ladles and spoons. In later years, horns were hollowed out and made into containers for gunpowder.

On the upper Missouri River, buffalo hides were used for small, tub-shaped boats. Sioux and Mandan women crossed rivers in personal boats made from circles of hide stretched over willow frames. These bullboats were light enough for women to carry on their backs.

Another important resource was stone. Stone was essential to people all over the continent. Soft stone, such as soapstone, was used to make pipe bowls, dishes, and other containers. Harder stone, such as flint and **obsidian**, was chipped into shape. Craftsmen used bone chisels to chip small flakes off a rock. The chipped stone was usually quite sharp at the edges. This is how arrowheads and stone axes were made.

Like their neighbors to the north, natives of Southeastern America and the Great Plains used bows and arrows to hunt and make war. Fighting was a constant part of life in the Southeast. In fact, the Cherokee once claimed, "We cannot live without war." Their **quivers** and bow cases were decorated skins and hides stitched together.

Most men in the area wore their hair short so as not to interfere with their bowstrings. They used sharp shells to cut their hair. Some shaved their heads on one side only. Choctaw men were an exception. They wore their hair long despite their use of bows and arrows.

During early times, warriors carried large shields and long bows. They wore rawhide armor to deflect enemies' arrows. Horseback riding changed all that. Shields and bows got smaller to make riding easier. Since swift movement was so important, warriors got rid of their bulky armor and fought wearing little clothing. Sioux warriors found a unique way to save space. They put a spear point on the upper

Native American women used the bullboat, which consisted of a buffalo hide stretched over a willow frame, to cross rivers.

27

end of their bows, which they used in hand-to-hand combat, instead of carrying a second weapon.

Plains Indians also used composite clubs. Composite clubs have a wooden handle and a head made of something else. Many clubs were fitted with stone spikes. The stone-headed club was the main weapon on the Plains until whites brought metal. On the Northwestern Plains, the Flathead tribe used a different kind of composite club, called a *pogamoggan*. It had a bag attached to the head. Inside the bag was a stone, making the weapon even deadlier. ⑨

Weirs, fence-like enclosures built across streams, trapped fish so that Native Americans could easily catch them.

 **Tools and Weapons of the Northwest**

The Northwestern United States was one of the richest areas on the continent. Natural resources were abundant, and there was always plenty of food to eat. Native Americans filled their bowls with salmon, herring, cod, and halibut. The Chinook people used basket traps and **weirs** to catch salmon on the lower Columbia River. Fish trapped in a weir were then speared.

The Tsimshian people used rakes and funnel-shaped nets to catch eulachon. Eulachon are small, oily fish. They are sometimes called candlefish, because when dried they can be lit like a candle. In fact, they are so oily that they burn for hours.

The people of the lower Northwest coast were skilled at woodworking. To shape and carve wood, they used axes, chisels, knives, hammers, and wedges. Some tools were made of bone or antler. Others were made of hard stone, such as serpentine or jade.

Northwest men used harpoons to hunt sea mammals. Harpoons are spears with rope attached. The rope lets the hunter pull his prey back to the boat. In 1803, the Nootka people took a big step in harpoon making. Using English guns, the Nootka raided an English ship and stole enough iron to make iron harpoons. This resulted in

one of their most successful whale-hunting seasons ever.

As in the Southeast, natives of the lower Northwest coast used dugouts for hunting and travel. Trails in the area were rough and often overgrown with vines, which made overland trips difficult.

The Haida people made the best dugouts in the region. Their dugouts were cut from red cedar trees and waterproofed with asphalt. Asphalt is a sticky mixture of tar, gravel, and sand. Haida dugouts were sometimes 50 feet long and 8 feet wide. They could hold up to 60 men and could carry nearly three tons. The Haida traded their dugouts with many tribes along the coast.

A group of Inuit set out for a hunting trip in an umiak. These open boats, which might reach 30 feet in length, were useful in hunting whales and walruses.

As large as Haida dugouts were, they could be made even larger. Sometimes, Haida men lashed two dugouts together. They would install a plank deck between the boats, making the dugouts into a war ship.

Other tribes did similar things for a peaceful reason. Houses were moved to the ocean shore each spring for herring season. The boards of houses would be lashed to two canoes, making a

Snowshoes, invented by Native Americans, help distribute a person's weight over a larger surface and thus prevent the person from sinking into deep snow.

temporary raft. With the family's belongings piled on top, the raft was ready to float downriver.

Further north, the dugout gave way to the **kayak** and umiak. The Tlingit people in Yakutat Bay used both types of boats. Although used for sports today, a kayak is a hunting boat. It is fast and silent, perfect

had
the
irst.
uns
ivals.

ee
ttle.
vely.

to

nd

ack
te:

"Their former weapons, Bows and Arrows, Spears
and Clubs, are now thrown aside and forgotten.
At Nootka, everyone had his musket."

Rifles were even distributed by the U.S.
government for buffalo hunting. Still, many
tribes used bows and arrows for the hunt. They
were quieter and more accurate. However, the
gun remained the prized weapon of war. Some
warriors even held bullets in their mouths to
cut down reloading time.

NATIVE AMERICAN LIFE

for sneaking up on resting seals. The kayak was also useful in chasing swimming caribou across a river.

The kayak was made by stretching sealskin over a frame pieced together with driftwood and antlers. The boat's pilot would fit into a small hole that pressed tight against his body. This kept water out of the craft. The sealskin was kept waterproof by regularly treating it with animal oils.

The kayak was light enough for one man to carry. This made it perfect for traveling overland as well as through the water. A skilled kayaker could paddle around seven miles per hour, even in rough water.

Unlike the kayak, an umiak is an open boat. Umiaks can be up to 30 feet long and can carry more than a ton of weight. Umiaks were used to hunt whales and walrus—prey that needed a group of men to be subdued. Umiaks are covered in hides. These hides are nearly as tough as wood, but they are more pliable. A wooden boat might break if it hit an ice floe. With the hide covering, there is less chance of serious damage if this happens.

In the frozen Arctic, natural resources are scarce, as it is too cold for trees to grow. The people of this region used every last scrap of what they had to survive. Their only source of wood was driftwood from the south. Arctic tools were made of stone, bone, or driftwood. It didn't matter what material was best for each tool. When someone needed an axe, he used what was handy to make one.

Like people in other regions, Arctic tribes used bows and arrows. Their bows were antler and driftwood lashed together with sinew. They would be backed with sealskin and braids of caribou sinew for strength. Their arrows were usually tipped with bone.

Dogs pull Mandan sledges across a frozen lake in this 1834 illustration.

Many tools were made from parts of animals. Bone, antler, and tusks were made into sharp tools, like spears, needles, and knives. Inuit women used a moon-shaped knife called an *ulu* to cut skins and fish.

Skins and hides were important, as was an animal's oil. Aleuts used lamps filled with oil from sea mammals. They were lit with bird down and dry grass as a wick. Some lamps could be laid flat to warm the person standing above them.

One of the most ingenious hunting tools used in the Arctic was the "death pill." This was used for hunting wolves. The hunter coiled up some whalebone. Then, he froze the bone into a ball of whale blubber. He would leave it out for wolves to eat. When a wolf ate the ball, the frozen blubber would begin to thaw. When it did, the whalebone sprung open, killing the wolf from inside.

Another useful hunting tool was a bit of swan's down. This was used when hunting seals under a sheet of ice. Seals are mammals, so they need air to breathe. A hunter would hang the down over a seal's breathing hole. He would watch the down very carefully. When the down moved, it meant the seal was under the hole. Then the hunter would drive his spear through the ice, killing the seal without ever seeing it.

When hunting at sea, hunters used sealskin floats called *avatuks*. There was usually a rope on either end of the *avatuk*. During a seal hunt, the *avatuk* would be tied to the dead seals to keep them from floating away. *Avatuks* were also tied to harpoon lines during whale hunts and were used as life preservers. An *avatuk* could keep someone afloat while he patched his kayak.

The Netsilik people on Canada's Kellet River attracted fish by lowering a lure into the water. A lure could be skin from a salmon's belly or a piece of bone carved in the shape of a fish. When the fish arrived, the fisherman would slowly raise the lure to the surface. When the fish was in range, he would spear it with a leister.

Due to the freezing climate, overland travel was difficult. Many tribes, including the Tlingits, added spikes to their snowshoes. Modern mountain climbers call these spikes crampons. They make it easier to walk on ice without slipping. Another safety tool was the test staff. This was a stick about the size of a ski pole. It was useful for poking uncertain patches of ice to make sure they could support a person's weight.

Dogs pulled sleds made of wood or hide with whalebone runners. The runners were supported with crosspieces made from caribou antlers. Strips of rawhide absorbed the shock of bumps in the ice. Some sleds' runners were made of stiff rawhide. These were coated with a mix of frozen clay and moss. The coating made them last longer and smoothed them out for an easier ride. ⑤

37

NATIVE AMERICAN LIFE

This Navajo blanket depicts two
holy spirits with a maize (corn)
plant, considered sacred by some
peoples of the Southwest.

 **Tools and Weapons of the Southwest**

The most important tool in the Southwest could not be held in the hand. In the desert, the thing people needed most was water.

The Hohokam people solved this problem nearly 2,500 years ago. The Hohokam were experts at water management. This was necessary to survive the dry Arizona climate. Every drop of water counted. Their solution was irrigation. Irrigation is a way to bring water to farmland through a series of channels. The Hohokam people dug wide, shallow irrigation canals from the Salt and Gila Rivers. Their oldest surviving canal was dug in 300 B.C. and is three miles long. Some canals were three times that size. Water flowed through them to the farmland. The Hohokam grew corn, beans, squash, tobacco, and cotton.

To support their canals, the Hohokam built dams on the Gila and Salt Rivers. These dams were a row of posts stuck into the riverbed. Between the posts, the Hohokam set woven mats. The mats blocked the water, making the river level rise. This meant that more water would flow into the canals. They could add or remove mats as necessary.

The Hohokam settled in Snaketown, near where Phoenix is today. Snaketown was abandoned in the early 16th century. No one knows for sure what happened to the Hohokam. They may be the ancestors of the modern-day Pima and Papago Indians, who inherited their system of irrigation canals.

Farther west, in California, natives were using decoys to attract ducks by 2500 B.C. They would make a frame out of tule reeds and cover it with strips of yucca. It would be decorated with paint and feathers. A hunter would wait in the reeds near the decoy. He would make tiny splashes in the water. It would sound like a duck was feeding there. When a real duck came, the hunter would leap out and grab it.

As time went on, new tribes migrated into the Southwest. The Apache lived as nomadic hunters. They used lances and bows made of willow branches. Their arrows were made from reeds with flint arrowheads. They also used war clubs and slings. Boys mostly used slings, since they were not strong enough to kill. Young Apaches trained with arrows. They practiced shooting, as well as dodging, them.

Most Apache battles were surprise attacks. This was not unusual among Southwestern tribes. Pueblo warriors would strike with surprise at dawn, then retreat quickly. They were outfitted with arrows, clubs, stone knives, and a bag of roasted cornmeal for trail food. Natives of southern California used daggers made from elk antlers. They had no edge to them, just a point at the tip. A leather strap was attached that could be wrapped around the wrist.

A Native American in California created this basket from willow leaves woven together.

Unlike the Apache, the Navajo took up the agricultural life of the neighboring Pueblos. They learned farming and weaving from the Pueblos in the 1600s. Only Southwestern Indians had true weaving looms. In every other region of North America, people were using finger weaving, knitting, and crocheting. Eventually, the Navajo became better weavers than their teachers. When Europeans brought sheep to America, Navajos began raising them for wool.

Natives of the region made cradleboards from wood and plant fibers. These were baby carriers worn on the parent's back. The baby's mother and grandmother usually covered them in decorations. Cradleboards were used throughout North America.

The Plano people had a tool for grinding seeds, a variation of which was used throughout the continent. The seeds were laid on a stone slab called a metate. A woman ground the seeds with a round stone known as a mano.

One of the most useful Native American crafts was pottery. Aside from those living in the Northwest, almost every native tribe made pottery. Pottery was used in cooking, storage, and even transportation. The people of the Southwest and Southeast are considered some of the best potters.

There is a long tradition of pottery in the Southwest. The Mogollon people of New Mexico made excellent pottery. They were careful, dedicated painters. One surviving Mogollon bowl has 27 parallel lines painted around it in a two-inch band.

There were two ways of shaping clay for pottery. Native Americans did not have potter's wheels. Like baskets, clay could be coiled and shaped. After the coils had been built into the right shape, the clay would be smoothed out.

The other method was to use a mold. In this case, a potter pressed clay up against a wooden mold, smoothing it out as she went. When the pot was finished, she removed the mold. The clay would keep its shape.

Most clay pots were dried by fire. The pots were placed above a

TANNING HIDES

Animal hides were important to Native Americans. In various regions, leather and rawhide provided clothing, shelter, tools, and transportation. Tanning is the process used to make animal flesh into a useful hide.

The most common method of tanning was brain tanning. To start, fresh hides were soaked in water. This was followed by a mixture of animal brains, liver, bark, and sour milk. After steeping in the mix, the hides would be wrung out and stretched over a frame to dry. This process made the hides soft and pliable. Next, hair would be scraped off the hides. The hides would be soaked in water regularly during the scraping, which kept them soft.

Drying was the final stage of tanning. It gave the leather color. Brown leather was dried over a fire of young, green willows. For yellow leather, the hides were dried over a dry willow fire. White leather was dried with no fire at all.

Hides that had the flesh and hair removed, but weren't tanned into leather, were called rawhide. Unlike leather, it was hard, sturdy stuff. It was used for shields and sometimes armor.

The Native Americans of the Southwest produced beautiful
pottery, like this finely decorated Hopi bowl.

fire. Above them was another, finished clay vessel. Inside it would be burning animal dung, which heated the top of the pot. When the firing was finished, the pots were left to cool. Eventually, they were decorated with designs of rabbits, turtles, and bears.

Since much of the Southwest was desert, there was not much need for boats. The Mohave used them only rarely. They swam across rivers, keeping their children afloat in clay pots. The Cocopa used these pots, too, calling them ollas. Since they lived on the banks of the Sea of California, they also used dugouts made of cottonwood.

Some California tribes, such as the Pomo Indians, used rafts made of tule reeds tied together. After a few hours of use, the rafts would become waterlogged and begin to sink. The warm California air dried the soggy rafts quickly, but they were not the most efficient form of boat.

The Chumash Indians of southern California used plank boats. These boats were made of hand-split planks, tied together with leather or fiber. The seams of the boat were sealed with asphalt to keep them waterproof. To this day, no complete Chumash plank boat has ever been found. §

Tools and Weapons of Central and South America

The Maya of Central America created one of the greatest civilizations in the Americas. An agricultural people, they were able to support cities by farming outlying areas. Mayan farmers cleared acres of forests by cutting down the native vegetation, allowing it to dry, and burning it. They use the ash as a fertilizer. In addition to the large fields that were cultivated, Mayan citizens kept gardens near their homes.

In the southern area of the Mayan world (in present-day Guatemala and Honduras), farmers had the opposite problem of farmers in the Southwest: too much rain. In some cases, Mayan farmers had to dig drainage canals to prevent their crops from being flooded.

A Mayan woman grinds corn as her people have done for centuries. Before the arrival of the Spanish in the 16th century, the Maya created a highly advanced culture in what is today Guatemala, Honduras, and the Yucatán Peninsula of Mexico.

Although the Mayans used metals, they did not use them for tools. They considered the metals too precious for anything but ceremony and decoration. Chisels, manos, metates, and bark beaters were made out of stone. A bark beater was a pounding tool used to soften bark. Bark fiber softened in this way was turned into paper for Mayan books.

Some of the finest tools were made from jade. Because jade is so hard, it is difficult to shape. Jade was cut by repeatedly rubbing cords across the spot that needed cutting. The cords would be wet with abrasives, such as sand. The constant rubbing eventually ground the jade down.

Mayan weavers used a variation on the loom called the belt loom. One end of it would be tied to a tree. The other end would be tied to the weaver's belt. The weaver could lean in to the tree to loosen the **warp** and lean out to tighten it. Baskets and sleeping mats were common woven items in Mayan households.

Mayans fished with bone fishhooks and nets weighed down with fired clay. They used dugouts to travel the waterways. Mayans hunted with bows, spears, and traps. They hunted deer, monkeys, **tapir**, birds, and rabbits. Snares were used for hunting deer.

In the 12th and 14th centuries, two great empires were founded in Central and South America. First, the Inca Empire grew in the Andes Mountains. Different provinces of the Inca Empire specialized in different weapons. Soldiers from these areas used their own weapons as well as the equipment the Incas supplied them with.

In the forests, the Antisuyus used bows and arrows. The tribes along the Ecuadorian coast preferred spears and darts. Men from the Colla

Tools and ornaments of a
South American hunter.

province were experts with **bolas**. A bola consisted of three stones tied to cords, which were then tied together. Soldiers threw them at their opponents' feet. The stones and cords would loop around legs, tripping people. They were also useful at snaring a deer's legs on a hunt.

The Incas provided all the tribes under their control with slings, called **huaracas**. When not being used, the slings could be tied around soldiers' waists like belts. The Incas also provided their army with spears and war clubs.

One example of an Incan war club is the star-headed mace. This was a composite club with a circular head made of stone or metal. There were six nubs sticking out of it, making the head look like a star.

Incas also used battle-axes with stone and bronze heads. Their spears had metal tips or wooden points hardened by fire. In later years, Incas used spears mostly for rituals.

When the Incas went to war, not everyone on the field was a soldier. The Incan army brought along a band, which played war songs full of boasting and insults to their enemy. Musicians played flutes made of bone, trumpets made of clay and shells, and tambourines made from the skins of their enemies.

Battles would begin with soldiers using their slings at long range. As the armies closed in, archers shot arrows at each other. Finally, clubs and spears were used in hand-to-hand combat. Shields were used for defense.

In the 14th century, the Aztec Empire began in central Mexico. The Aztecs used similar weapons, with a few variations. Aztecs used bows and cotton slings for their long-range attacks. The slings threw egg-sized stones. Aztec bows were around five feet long. The arrows were tipped with bone or obsidian (volcanic glass) or were simply fire-hardened.

Aztecs also used the javelin, a type of spear. To throw their javelins farther, the Aztecs used a tool called an **atlatl**. It was a stick around two feet long with a peg at one end to hold the spear in place. On the other end was a handle made from shells. A soldier would hold it and swing his arm back to throw. The atlatl extended the length of the soldier's arm, which made the spear fly farther.

NATIVE AMERICAN METALWORK

Until European contact, metal wasn't used in North America. Tools were made from stone, bone, or wood. When Europeans came, natives of both coasts saw the strength of metal and traded for metal of all kinds. Tools could be used immediately. Brass buttons could be remade into jewelry or other things.

In this way, metal took the place of many traditional stone tools. Stone axes and bone needles were replaced by metal versions. As metal cookware become more common, the demand for pottery shrank.

During this time, Native Americans also discovered the power of guns. Once this happened, the demand for metal went down. Guns and ammunition were their main demand when trading. Tribes cut their gun barrels short and used the extra iron to make metal tools. By the early 1800s, metal was found in many North American tools.

In Central and South America, things were different. Metal was common there, and metalworking was an art. Although the Maya used metals, they only rarely used them for tools. The most common metals in the area were gold, silver, and copper. They are soft metals that can't take much punishment. As a result, metal was mostly used for religious items, such as bracelets, masks, and other ritual objects.

The Incas were quite knowledgeable about the properties of metals. They knew how the strength of bronze changed with the amount of tin it contained. Thus, their bronze tools were superior to the stone ones used before them.

The bola served as both a weapon of war and a hunting tool in parts of the Inca Empire. Here, South American cowboys of the 19th century use bolas to hunt a rhea, a flightless bird similar to the ostrich.

At close range, Aztecs would use a special two-handed sword called a **macana**. It was heavy and made of hard wood. The sides were edged with shards of obsidian. When broken, obsidian is extremely sharp. Spanish records say the *macana* was so sharp that it could be used to chop the head off a horse. These swords were very effective when they were first made. However, unlike metal, obsidian turns dull quickly. Thus, the swords needed to be resharpened regularly.

To protect themselves, Aztec warriors wore thick armor made of quilted cotton soaked in brine. The armor was effective, especially against spears and arrows. When the Spanish invaded, they began using the cotton armor as well. Their metal armor was too heavy and hot for the climate.

Soldiers also used small round shields strapped to their forearms. This kind of shield is called a **buckler**. They were between 20 and 30 inches wide and were made of wooden rods laced together with cotton. Fancier shields were decorated with gold or turquoise.

The Incas were more advanced farmers than the Aztecs. Aztecs used digging sticks, which were a combination of a spade and a hoe. The Incas used a foot plow called a *taclla*. It was a six-foot-long pole with a digging point. There was a footrest near the point and a handle on the top. Farmers bore down on the footrest with their weight to make digging easier.

Incan farmers also used handheld hoes called **quranas**. *Quranas* had a short shaft with a blade like a chisel. Some of these tools had wooden blades. The better-made ones used bronze. Incan farmers had a special tool to break up lumps of earth. They also used a boat-shaped board for scraping soil over planted seeds.

The Jivaro Indians of Ecuador used similar tools. Jivaro women planted and harvested. They grew bananas, peanuts, sugar cane, and manioc. They used sharp, pointed planting sticks and flat-bladed digging sticks. Men used machetes to clear an area for farming.

The Jivaro of South America hunted
monkeys and birds with blowguns made
from ivory nut palm leaves. By blowing
into the tube, the hunter would propel a
poison-tipped dart at his prey.

To round out their diet, the Jivaro hunted anaconda, toucans, monkeys, and armadillos. They used a double-edged dagger with a point at both ends and a handle in the center. To hunt birds and monkeys, they used blowguns. Jivaro blowguns are long tubes made from ivory nut palm leaves. They shoot light darts, propelled by a puff of breath. The darts are poisoned, usually with curare. Curare is a deadly muscle-relaxing poison made from tropical plants.

The Jivaro poison blowgun is one of the most extreme examples of ingenuity in Native American toolmaking. It makes a tube out of one plant and a dart from the stem of another, which is coated with a poison from a third plant. Native Americans have always found effective uses for their environment. Their tools and weapons are evidence that long before Henry Ford, Alexander Graham Bell, and Thomas Edison, the Americas were home to brilliant inventors. ⑤

CHRONOLOGY

400 B.C. Mayan civilization begins.

300 B.C. Hohokam people build early irrigation canals in Arizona.

A.D. 1100s The Inca establish their capital at Cuzco.

1325 Aztecs found their capital city, Tenochtitlán.

1492 Christopher Columbus sails to America in search of Asia.

1500s Hohokam people abandon Snaketown.

1521 Spanish capture Tenochtitlán, conquering the Aztecs.

1532 Spanish conquer the Inca.

1620 Pilgrims settle at Plymouth, Massachusetts.

1626 The Dutch buy Manhattan Island from the Native Americans.

Late 1600s Plains Indians begin to get horses.

1670 Guns first traded to Native Americans on Hudson Bay.

1778 Northwest tribes begin trade with Captain James Cook of England.

1803 Nootkas raid an English ship for metal and use it to make harpoons.

1804 U.S. government enacts the Louisiana Territory Act, which tries to move Southeastern Indians west of the Mississippi River.

1812 War of 1812 begins. Most Indians side with the British.

1813–1814 The Creeks declare war on the United States, resulting in the loss of 22 million acres to the U.S. government.

1830 U.S. government passes the Indian Removal Act. Southeastern Indians are moved over the "Trail of Tears" to Oklahoma.

1867 United States buys Alaska.

1876 On June 25, General George Custer and his troops are killed by Sioux and Cheyenne warriors at the Battle of Little Bighorn.

1890 In December, the Seventh Cavalry kills 150 Sioux men, women, and children at Wounded Knee, South Dakota.

2013 Recent government statistics indicate that there are more than 5.2 million Native Americans living in the United States and Canada.

GLOSSARY

adze a scraping tool made out of stone or bone.

atlatl an Aztec spear-throwing device used to increase a spear's range.

bola a thrown snaring weapon made of stones and cords.

buckler a small round shield strapped to the forearm.

huaraca an Incan sling that could be tied around the waist like a belt.

kayak a one-man boat used in the Arctic with an enclosed seat for the pilot.

leister a three-pronged spear.

macana a heavy wooden sword edged with shards of obsidian.

makuk a birch bark basket used in the Northeast for gathering crops.

mattock a bladed digging tool similar to a pick.

obsidian black volcanic glass.

quiver a case for holding or carrying arrows.

qurana an Incan hoe with a short shaft and a blade like a chisel.

rawhide untanned hides of cattle.

sinew animal tendon.

tapir a pig-like animal found in the rain forests of Central and South America.

warp a series of yarns extended lengthwise in a loom and crossed by the weft.

weir a fence or enclosure set in a waterway for taking fish.

FURTHER READING

Burch, Monte. *Making Native American Hunting, Fighting, and Survival Tools: The Complete Guide*. Guilford, Conn.: The Lyons Press, 2007.

Fichter, George S. *How to Build an Indian Canoe*. New York: David McKay Company, Inc., 1977.

Harding, David, ed. *Weapons: An International Encyclopedia from 5000 B.C. to A.D. 2000*. New York: St. Martin's Press, 1980.

Jennings, Matthew. *New Worlds of Violence: Cultures and Conquests in the Early American Southwest*. Knoxville: University of Tennessee Press, 2011.

Kavin, Kim. *Tools of Native Americans: A Kid's Guide to the History and Culture of the First Americans*. White River Junction, Vt.: Nomad Press, 2006.

MacQuarrie, Kim. *The Last Days of the Incas*. New York: Simon and Schuster, 2007.

Waldman, Carl. *Encyclopedia of Native American Tribes*. New York: Facts on File, 2006.

NATIVE AMERICAN LIFE

INTERNET RESOURCES

http://www.csulb.edu/colleges/cla/departments/americanindianstudies/faculty/trj

Website of the American Indian Studies program at California State
University, Long Beach, which is chaired by Professor Troy Johnson. The site
presents unique artwork, photographs, video, and sound recordings that
accurately reflect the rich history and culture of Native Americans.

http://www.kstrom.net/isk/mainmenu.html

This web site contains extensive resource material on Native Americans.

http://www.nativeweb.org/resources

This web site features a collection of resources and links to informative
Native American Web sites.

http://nmai.si.edu/home/

This site contains fascinating information collected by the Smithsonian
Institution about Native American history and culture.

NATIVE AMERICAN LIFE

INDEX

NATIVE AMERICAN LIFE

PICTURE CREDITS

CONTRIBUTORS

Dr. Troy Johnson is chairman of the American Indian Studies program at California State University, Long Beach, California. He is an internationally published author and is the author, co-author, or editor of twenty books, including *Wisdom Spirits: American Indian Prophets, Revitalization Movements, and Cultural Survival* (University of Nebraska Press, 2012); *The Indians of Eastern Texas and The Fredonia Revolution of 1828* (Edwin Mellen Press, 2011); and *The American Indian Red Power Movement: Alcatraz to Wounded Knee* (University of Nebraska Press, 2008). He has published numerous scholarly articles, has spoken at conferences across the United States, and is a member of the editorial board of the journals *American Indian Culture and Research* and *The History Teacher*. Dr. Johnson has served as president of the Society of History Education since 2001. He has won awards for his permanent exhibit at Alcatraz Island; he also was named Most Valuable Professor of the Year by California State University, Long Beach, in 1997 and again in 2006. He served as associate director and historical consultant on the award-winning PBS documentary film *Alcatraz Is Not an Island* (1999). Dr. Johnson lives in Long Beach, California.

Rob Staeger lives and writes near Philadelphia. A former newspaper editor, he has written many short stories for young people and several plays for older ones. He has written several nonfiction books, including *Wyatt Earp*, *The Boom Towns*, and *Games of the Native Americans*.